Chaos and Bloom

A.M. JOHNSON

Chaos and Bloom
accompanied with
A Hypochondriac's Notebook
A.M. JOHNSON
ISBN 978-1-7320842-1-6

Editing & Formatting by Elaine York,
Allusion Graphics, LLC, www.allusiongraphics.com
Cover Design by Bex Harper

Chaos and Bloom

For You
And all that you are
Color, Sound, Verse
Beautiful bird
Words are your freedom

Inside us all is a written page, a fiction that burns and devours. Embrace each word, swallow them, and become the one thing you've always wanted to be.

Dear Reader,

Words have always been a way for me to cope. Cope with life. A friend of mine once said we bleed our souls onto paper. As a writer, I give you a piece of myself with every syllable, and even though I find that fiction is a place for me to lose the hardships of life, poetry has always been my number one outlet.

This book is divided up into my earlier work (seedling) and will lead into the poetry I am currently writing today. My earlier work is messy, but it's real.

I was young—a teenager—dealing with a crazy-as-hell childhood. I was trying to understand who I was, understand boys and distinguish between their love versus lust, and I hope as you read this, you see a bit of yourself reflected in the words.

I've also included *A Hypochondriac's Notebook*, previously published in the now out-of-print anthology, *Begin Again*. Intended to be a fictitious biography about a girl named Anna Josh, most of the writing delves into a memoir I'd worked on in my earlier years and ended up rearranging for actual publication...

If you never had a chance to read it, now is your chance.

Thank you for taking this journey with me,

Much love,
Amanda Johnson

LOAM

#1

your eyes
muse to my heart smile
lips, soft sadness
I can taste it
let's forget the strings
mute the music
for our own feverish sound
wanting more of it
I will find you

#2

I like it here with you
gently kissing time into tomorrow
a lightness comes with it
as segments of daydreams
bring a smile to your lips
this new discovery
sends chills
as your fingertips touch my skin
our hands find each other
and your dark eyes listen to mine

#3

nervous laughter
unsteady hands
stomach aches with a happy sickness
an embrace
it felt right
to be your music
to be your favorite song
for you to hear what I am feeling
slow burning smoke
curls and sleeps inside me
still, you were there
and all you gave me
was your smile

#4

there's this sickness
and it breathes down my throat
it coaxes me to think in a certain way
where everything you do is perfect
and your eyes shine
until I no longer feel my loss
and my heart is bound
I feel wanted and owned
but stale and overused
there is this disease
and it flows through my veins
it molds each heartbeat as yours
it creates a picture, an image divine
but my skin is loose
I feel formed and fake
and the blurred likeness glorified
without the words
I will dissolve

#5

nothing truly defines her
she's not some boxed-up bubble gum
chewed up
forgotten masterpiece
displayed for your pleasure
she's a reality
an imperfectly gorgeous phenomenon
she's the spark
the palace
the beginning
she's destruction
chaos and bloom
she's a belief
a stunning dedication
an ever-pressing reminder
in the end
without her
you are lost

#6

I have survived the war
I have surrendered
with a heart that aches
for a love that will stop at nothing
a mind tired with anxiety
and eyes
eyes so heavy and unseen
this brilliant world, swirling
with anticipation greets me
tonight
I sleep alone
and truly I sleep
for once
he was no longer my prescription

#7

liar heart
you can't keep me still
all I had
it was yours
twisted by the faith
the ideal
by your touch
I'm stuck
I'm weak
I'm gone
a faint voice
a calm before the raging tide
you can't hold this
you can't fix it
all I've been, it was ours
dissected by the verse
the moment, your eyes
I'm afraid
I'm alone
I'm lost

#8

shudder to the touch, I sink
I can picture you
unread and unknown
such perfection for my purity
drab and dusty are these sheets I bear
every word you speak snips another square
this sheet dwindles
my naked body lies
air surrounds my silhouette
cold, a shiver runs up my spine
closing my eyes, I feel new
warm hands that mold and form
eyes defiant
I do nothing more
crumbling innocence
I've stepped into your sanctuary

#9

rooted down underneath my insignificant skin. my mumbled overtures and sarcastic gestures have come on like a fire within a cup of digested alcohol. the sneered comments all fly around my distracted brown bag of a brain. my voice falls to the muggy tile floor. beige squares of my life, the grout, each line, a history, weaving through the smug and cigarette-stained walls. thinking you're the father figure of my dreams, the daddy I'll never have... go back to your happy little household. take your pink-bunnied, sheep-bearing wallpaper and grow yourself. reach past my meaningful life, and find one of your own.

#10

the river flows fast through the mental disruption
inspiration like medicine
rips through sadness
like the madman freed
into a world that has become different
he is lost
like the tears of a mother
who cries
to find that her creation is dying

SEEDLING

#11

dewdrop sunshine
tastes timeless
as rose petals dance on fingertips
while daisies dollop on river lake water shine

#12

she takes toll in breath
and silence on walks
dreams of heavens as daylight passes
forever so far away
to touch the sun with her fingertips
takes a journey to the horizon
petals fall like rain to touch her cheeks
and turns them to rose
warmth like a blanket
covers quickly
blue clouds and white skies
a perfect daisy dances on her toes
breeze by my life
help me find my solace
show me where to go

#13

nicotine, nicotine, despised breath
crawl up and fall down beneath this wretched bed
boredom slides slowly through my veins
sickness in my belly
my eyes want to creep out
into the midnight sky
this prison keeps me
smothered under sheets
I need a quick fix of laughter
of life
of you

#14

she sits
common
divine
breath like a cloud
seeps slowly into souls
her words wander
on tulip tips
creative concoctions
give delusions of pleasure
wishing on a star
she falls
deep, dank
into her own destruction
and stumbles seductively
to a poisoned sleep

#15

there is no security in yes
no happiness in yesterday
today is never here
and I have forgotten the truth

#16

who is this mysterious man
this artic chill
understanding the deep sadness beneath my sheets
private, sincere with cold eyes
who is this heaviness
slow beating breaks against my skin
mental show
with glass doors
but he denies me the key
spectacle of a beautiful scene
like stars in an open winter sky
he is my honesty
silence
breath heaving breasts
he is my tranquility

#17

these days the picture is focused
and he is the lens
her image
a reel of movement and emotion
no longer a picture of what could have been

#18

taken by the light
sound of the sun
and how it breathes onto my skin
like the heat of your palm
on my belly
when I felt like yours
and I thought
you were mine
like the lies were music
and I'd always remember
the sound of you singing

#19

tell me I'm beautiful
my flaws are yours
and I'll see you across the room
with a drink in your hand
and a dimple in your five o'clock shadow
your half smile, a cage to capture
as you stand
with your hand in your pocket
waiting for the kill

#20

make me feel delicate
I whispered
right before he broke me

ROOTS

#21

if loss is a star in the pitch night sky
then yours burns the brightest
and will never die

#22

weight
pushes and cracks
sternum splits
lungs fill
doubt devours and pressure drowns
those eyes of yours
do nothing to help
vacant, void syllables part his lips
tired and cold
these dark sides of you
selfish and alone
begging to scream
to let go

#23

there was no hope in her
she was full of shadows
and the gray light of dawn
was just an illusion
sick with the perversion of her truth

#24

the horses have come home
gold and sharp
hands reaching
for the reins
until it tasted bitter
infatuated with the race
the dusted path away
from this tiny blue house
where the horses cry
for the gravel and grit
of the fast escape

#25

mistress
take this bottle
and pour it in your lap
as your fingertips measure my ribs
as the wall measures my spine
and your teeth memorize my lips
your voice
stolen syllables
I'll keep
as the taste of your mouth
writes itself on paper
conjured and unknown
simple lines
the distance
an unspeakable shield
and to know you
is to have you

#26

you deserve
soft words
and hot hands
midnight lips
that taste like dreams
caramel and sex
messy limbs
that hold your secrets
and the sounds you make
just for him

#27

snake in his nest
sweet tongues
disappear
until he needs
takes
lies to feed
dusting me in deep blue shades
of apathy

#28

the silent hand on my throat
keeps me from bleeding
from spilling my words
the ache only gifts
narrow sips of air
and my chest is a cage
for a heart too big
and lungs that refuse to move
I'm concrete
cold
in this bed
unsure and gray
wishing to sink to the bottom
this distance between me and them
me and you
between night and day
disappear
into the dark blue of forgetting
and find a way to breathe again

#29

"you have no heart," he said, and the words shredded my skin.

"you have it in your hands." I begged. "it still beats, can't you feel it?"

he shook his head.

my soul in all its fragments dripped down my cheeks as he turned and said in a dark whisper, "what I once held has no feeling anymore, there is no life in the air we breathe."

#30

do not fear the wreckage of love
there is no shame in the darkness
that smooths
your broken edges
or in the light of longing
that drips
along the cracks of your heart

BRANCHES

#31

inside my marrow
is dust
it crushes and forms
it bleeds and is reborn
in him
his heated grip
it presses
pulls
lingers in the air
and all the creases
where he took me that night
when everything was quiet and still
loud and screaming inside my head
the secret
he felt it before I spoke
and his eyes won every inch of me
his lips every taste
my heart molded within the bones
I was his creation

#32

he was battle and madness
she drank from his cup
desiccated
sipped the silver lined compliments
until she no longer could taste
her own despair

#33

the sound of you
haunting
flat against my chest
and whole inside my skin
the music of you
still plays

#34

there is the real you
harsh and cold
dripping with green
wishing to be silver
and wrapped around their fingers

#35

because she was weary with always
and couldn't find an eternity to worship
until him
he was the forever after
the plan of salvation
in his kiss
she found her religion

#36

he is starving. his hands worship the feast. taking all that he wants, I am left bare. unadorned, shuddering beneath his dark, ravenous gaze. the deep brown of his eyes drink me in from between my thighs. my hands tangle in his hair. his fingers lingering, punishing, slowly breaking me down, bringing me to the brink... he devours me.

#37

this waning heart forever wanders
trapped between resisting
and wanting

#38

wishing for the way that song makes me feel
how the guitar has me wanting things I'll never have
how I can almost feel him through the melodies
and he doesn't even exist

#39

loneliness is the raindrop
cascading down my dark window
falling for you in silver shades
as thunder rolls in heartbeats
when you kissed me
loneliness is the song
playing in the background
singing for you
in flat, soft verses
the drum, a breath
when you touched me
loneliness is the memory
stamped on the photo
smiling for you
in a bright dress of green
a shudder
across my skin
when you walked away

#40

"somedays it's hard to look in the mirror," she said as
the smoke curled from her lips and knotted around her
fingers.
left wanting, he drank her exhale, stealing her fragments
like a thief
keeping parts of her
inside his lungs
until he could show her
a reflection she could love

CHAOS

#41

disguise bruises her cheeks.
the light warm breeze catches the cloth
and billows in the dry air
berries tint her lips
full, inviting, blessed
to kiss them
to feel the heat
it's an unbridled fiction
a forfeited truth
she's absent inside the ending of her choices
longing for a moment that will never come

#42

deep color fills the horizon. it catches the leaves on fire with oranges and reds and golds. morning sunrise and you've left the window open. cool air smells sweet as it scatters across my sheets, and I'm grateful for the warmth that blankets my skin. grateful for the smile on your face as I look at you with sleep-painted eyes, grateful for this day and the promise it brings as you remind with a kiss how lucky I am to be here... with you.

#43

you put your hand in mine
and I felt it like the color yellow
like the last leaf, breaking free from the branch
burning orange
like the medicine that takes away the numb
I take you, drink you
like the memories I had weren't real
you dropped your hand
and the pocket of your jeans
like home to silence

#44

kissing you
in dreams
and reality wins
like the rain finds the soil
fleeting
until it's touched by the heat
of the morning sun

#45

I want to fall in love with you again
feel your hands on me for the first time
under covers
taste your mouth and its promises
feel more than vacant in your eyes
feel more like me
on the night the rules were broken
when the scent of relief filled our lungs
and tomorrow was more
than this commonplace car ride down streets
without trees and homes without life
I want to hear the melody
see beyond this everlasting beat
wake up sleep wake up sleep
keeping time till our end of days
I need a backup plan
a rescue route
I want to meet you again
in that dim light
lace our fingers until they sweat
remember the why of you
of us
and hold my beating heart before it breaks

#46

that dirty bass line
tattoos and three chord punch
dark eyes and butterflies
the beat of my heart
an angry hungry song
lips and leather
it's in my blood
fast kisses and hard touch
that guitar, those fingers
tobacco stained against my skin
"turn it up," he said.
and in the volume
I became his

#47

your grass wasn't greener
and her hands are still dirty
with the fine grit you've left behind
her skin a tainted reflection
of what she thought was more
than six o'clock dinner
electric bills and Saturday morning cartoons
the lie still prickles and puckers her flesh
the evidence, bruised fingerprints
a mark he'd never leave
not in a million years
or eight
this was a figment
a once upon a time
a fantasy for when she closed her eyes at night
in a silent house
and she was nothing more
than faded and washed and without

#48

she wanted tattoos
and rough fingertips
calloused words
and vicious kisses
she couldn't contain the darkness
no matter her sweet talk and shy eyes
he could feel it in her
the restless nature
the submission
she begged for understanding
despite the silence
and longing
her choice
revealed the ugly
and she put it all away
for now

#49

wishing for
his hands
two different realities
two different worlds
his eyes stare
and your heart hurts
wishing for the day you'll meet
two separate rooms
two separate speakers
same song
and he's wishing for you too

#50

there are parts of me that have never seen the sun
that will never see the color of light
its stunning spectrum
there are parts, dear friend, that tangle and knot
that ache and burn
parts so raw it hurts to touch
there are parts, dear friend, that only you will understand
that connect us in a beautiful misery
that deep twist
that forbidden dark
you see me
my soul in all its tiny, disassembled fragments
you've tasted them, and you've made them yours

BLOOM

#51

I am brave
for the knife you wield
those words
slice deep
but my armor is built
made strong by thick skin
and the solid bones you required
built on verse
melody, and sand-coated vocals
I am healed

#52

I love this light, the sound
it's grateful
it's precious in its perfection
the drums hammer through my earbuds
and the cabin pressure tightens my temples as I soar at
36,000 feet
I am infinite
the music calms and the wine shows me who I really am
deep beneath the everyday veneer, the drawn-up
blueprint of who the fuck I'm supposed to be
the self-hate evaporates
the love for the tune, each beat, each note, encapsulates
my heart... reminds me I love life, I love this moment,
this silly buzzed afterward, this timeless suspension
I feel it in each pore and, as I near the landing, I fear the
arrival... the inevitable return... to my reality

#53

I am fable and folly
guise and dazzling
I am lust and sex
simple and sinful
I am chance and repentance
hopeful and real
I am truth and logic
pure and admirable
I am love
just love
born of the stars and all their offerings
alive within the ink, and the heavy weight of the moon
dark and full
follow me
and I will bring you the galaxy

#54

I gave you everything
and you walked away
with full pockets
and an empty heart

#55

he decorates my lips with lies
pretty words kissed to the flesh
compliments shaped
into a breathless whisper
and an illusion crests in his moan
it's delicate the way he kills me
wounds made from rare syllables
love. promise. you.
and the sound of his voice
spilling my secret pieces is my undoing

#56

because there is nothing but you
with dark eyes, and careless lips
and a smile that makes me forget
that I hate you

#57

that unruly heart
you'll never catch her
even in the gauzy light of the morning
when her smile is the most real
she'll see you for what you are

#58

in a world of black and white
forgotten are those who love in color
and sleep in dreams of starlight

#59

you loved me
and I took it
knowing
your heart was a liar
and mine
an empty page
needy for your words

#60

that disguise he wears
it's for you
you and your mouth
your words
he dreams of shadows
and hidden corners
skirts and fingers
heels and silk
off limits and he loves it
loves you
as he whispers into your ear
"I was never here."

#61

I want love under canopies
beneath midnight
back packs and forest green
mud on our shoes
and salt in our hair
the sun evaporates into stones
to match our heat
to fix his lips to mine
and the leaves tickle our legs
as the wind blows
bringing us farther from home

#62

and, God, she'll never let herself be free of doubt, free of fear. she'd have to smile at the world, say 'fuck you' to the definition that holds her captive, but her throat folds, and all she'll ever see is the fault that cages her in.

#63

innocence is a kiss of starlight
on the pink cheeks of time
It begs forgiveness
for ever loving the sun

#64

there is no pleasure in watching
from the sidelines
like a wallflower almost in bloom
like the girl you wish he wanted
one breath
one step
from the safe line
she can dabble with the kings
but advises
never been
the one they admire
the taste they desire
she is an underestimated beauty
simple
delicate
her backbone easily bent
her love hardly spent
spectator
voyeur
she holds tight
patient
waiting
for her knight

#65

I'm that feeling, that warmth
it saturates
even with the distance
that surrounds me
I'm a gorgeous pallet
a simple treasure
she is light
she is fortune
I am wanderlust
blessed to find the path

Other Works

Continue reading for *A Hypochondriac's Notebook*

A Hypochondriac's Notebook

By A.M. Johnson

*A somewhat biographical account
of a girl named Anna Josh*

And then there was this girl...

A romantic mind sometimes feels things until there is no more softness. I've discovered this over the years. Poetic thought will bring bricks to your temples. Striving for something, living with passion so intoxicating that sleep becomes a dream, and to get up every day, put your shoes on, brush your teeth, eat, it becomes nothing, an empty, daily chore that holds no purpose. Why not lie in bed all day, be grease pits, smell bad until our teeth rot out?

Existence is.

I find some people live a life of mindless meandering.

"Hey, honey, what's for dinner, chicken or beef?"

Their dilemma, right? But yet they have happiness, and still I sit trying to better myself, hungry for a love like no other and knowledge of something extraordinary. Writing the world the way I want, me and my pen.

So this is how it started.

I grew up in a small town that slowly transformed into a concrete jungle of strip malls, quick marts, and fast food joints. An adolescence of convenient suburbia. Drawn out by neatly made cheeseburgers, only 59 cents. Life was never easy as a teenager. Whether you were the wealthy kid on the block with brand new Guess jeans, shiny new Doc Martin boots, or just a middle-class girl with hand-me-down baggage and a thrift store T-shirt. The latter was my life. I never kept up with the Jones's, I only hoped that they wouldn't call the police again for yet another "domestic disturbance."

I can't complain too much, pain is relative. I always had what I needed regardless of the dysfunctional disaster I once called home. My mother fought hard for my family, taking on two jobs. She took all the blunt force physically and emotionally. She sacrificed her bones, her soul, and her flesh. Needless to say, you've figured out by now, that I had that archetypal, abusive father. Charming and funny. Everyone loved him and, I have to admit, I had as well, but he'd been just as good at inflicting pain as he'd been at telling jokes.

You should know, I'm the baby of multiple children. Big, blended family. His and hers and fists and alcohol. After a while, my mother sort of faded into the dreary, amber whiskey and chipped ice of her tumbler, and my dad mellowed into a cool shade of paranoia that would look good on anyone.

But I still had to grow, still had a life to live, and lessons to learn inside the hurricane of an adult war. Adult problems, and adult pain...how could a child, a teenager, ever survive?

I barely did.

I won't mention names... I only want to invade my own privacy for today. But, if it wasn't for my best friend, I'm not sure I would've made it. If it wasn't for her parents who practically let me live in their home every weekend, I'm not sure I'd be sitting in this chair typing out stories, and poetry, and romance.

I was fifteen years old when I almost killed myself.

Almost.

No gory details needed, no glorification. It was the worst choice I almost made. It would've been a permanent solution to a temporary problem. A problem that died of heart failure at sixty-seven. A problem I'd forgiven before he passed away six weeks after my first son was born. My father had shaped and molded me. My mother? She'd painted my emotional canvas. My adolescence was hard granite. Stone days filled with black skies. But I made it.

I broke through.

I'm here.

Breathing and fucking happy.

Happiness has no real definition. It's what you make of it. I've learned that you can make life through anything. Like on those cold nights when the stars seem to envelop you, when giant rain drops splash against your skin, when the sunlight is so warm against your sheets it wakes you, or even if it's gray, and the clouds grant you soft, overcast sleep, life will find you.

My best friend answered the phone the night I wanted to die. The night when every star went out. When I couldn't see past my own self-preservation, my own fear. When I couldn't see the end, or even the beginning anymore. She'd talked me off that ledge.

Unfortunately, there would be more ledges, and more fires and more fear, but fuck, I'd just begun to live. I'd found great friends, and an even greater escape.

Music.

Words.

Boys.

All the coping skills I'd eventually master. I'd try new things, and learn I hate crowds. I'd rope my anxiety, still do, and fall in love *a lot*. And shit, I'd experienced all of that by the time I'd turned twenty-three. But now I'm thirty-eight and my journals are full of black ink and hard times. Filled with stories, and yesterday, and tomorrow. Filled with what I was and who I've become. My heart beats on every page, and I'm lucky to breathe in the air each word gives me as I write it. I'm lucky because I didn't die, because I stepped forward, because I gave in to life and fucking lived it. And now, when I look back, I'm glad I chose to start over. I'm grateful I didn't bring that sharp blade to my wrist because if I had, I wouldn't have this. I wouldn't have *him*.

Do you remember the first time you fell in love? Like real love. Not the check yes, check no boxes you filled out in seventh grade. I'm talking about the love that splits you open, that makes you sick—crazy, and eventually, if it was worth it, it made you bleed, metaphorically speaking, of course. It's chaos and disgusting and you'd sell a kidney to have it. It's part of the human experience. It's part of the ride we get to live. We turn ourselves inside out and hope and pray that we'll find it, to be accepted so utterly by another human being.

When I was little I used to ride my tricycle in the garage with the door shut. I was so afraid of people, so much so that a two-car garage was plenty of space for a bike ride. Kids were cruel, and when you were the one in the neighborhood with the "crazy family" you learned the definition of introvert pretty damn quickly. Even at five, I knew the fear of acceptance. Maybe it was because I was brought up with aggression that made me seek out men who were passive. Too passive. Videogame loving, punk rockers who barely had time to dust their vinyl collection because they were too busy playing Dungeons & Dragons.

You see, I'd created coping mechanisms to survive. Only dated guys who couldn't hurt me. Men who would go with the flow. For years, I'd hid inside my little boat, and never, ever dared to rock it. The guys I wanted were easy, simple, casual, and generally dumped me for my best friend after we both realized we had no real connection. Well, they'd realize, I'd just get my heart tossed in the trash and eat a pile of fucking Oreos. But, the point...

Him...

It wasn't until I hit another rock bottom, walked another ledge that I was finally able to see what I was made of. The guy who brought me everything I never wanted, who shoved me into the fire and smiled as I burned, this story is why I find myself sitting here at four in the morning every night writing... creating... breathing.

Awake and Alive.

In the thick of it...
Fifteen years ago

The cigarette smoke curls around my lips and seeps into the air like a toxic snake. The room is foggy with fumes and heat and, as I lean against the counter, my elbows pushing into the glass, I can almost make out his silhouette from across the hall. The filtration system keeps in the smoke, making pungent clouds of carcinogenic veils I can barely see through. This smoke shop is the mall's one-stop shop for cancer and collectables. I've been selling knick-knacks, overpriced cigarettes and cigars for a year now. Last month, they actually promoted me to manager. The thought cracks through before I can stop it. Last month... the same month he started across the hall. His name? Torren Kruger. Occupation? He sells videogames at the used electronic store across from my shop.

I think I like him.

I like his dark hair, and smart mouth. His ability to take one simple statement and carve it into a thousand words that seem important and relevant. I like that he's shorter than I normally prefer, because he's cocky enough to pull it off. I'm a bit intrigued with his rough looking hands and how they belie his day job at a cash register. Suggesting when he's not pedaling the latest RPG he could be moving earth and stone. My ash falls to the counter and shakes me from my day drooling. I stamp the butt into the ceramic ashtray and glance back to the front windows of Electronic Garden. Torren's chin-length, chocolate brown hair is one of my favorite things about him, and I watch as he runs those well-worn hands through the lucky locks. I sigh. I actually fucking sigh like some love-sick teenager.

I definitely like him.

I like that he chooses my shop for his breaks instead of the food court. Preferring me and a nicotine buzz to food. If I close my eyes I could picture him on the other side of the counter. All smiles and jokes. Sharp and funny. That smile. It lights his face in a way I've never been privy to before. Happiness crinkles his skin and trickles past his lips with graveled laughter.

"Did you sleep last night?" his deep voice, familiar and warm, opens my eyes.

My laugh is nervous as I stand to my full height. Surprise feeds my pulse, it's not his usual break time. "Not really," I say with shy syllables and pink cheeks.

My eyes drink him in as he reaches into his pocket and pulls out a pack of Marlboro Reds. He's wearing a forest green polo, untucked with baggy, gray cargo pants. His jaw is tight as he pinches the cigarette between his teeth and lights it. My gaze falls to his long fingers and something inside my stomach breaks open. Swarms of butterflies spread throughout the hollow of my gut and my mouth goes dry.

He affects me.

I shake my head and push away from the counter.

"Out late?" he asks as his free hand runs through that thick hair again. My eyes catch on the black leather cuff he wears on his left wrist. It's new.

"Couldn't sleep."

He chuckles. "You never sleep."

My lips part involuntarily into a wide grin. He remembered.

He's right, I don't sleep. I hardly get more than two hours. I've been fighting dreams and the stars and the night sky for almost a year. My best friend thinks it's because I need to see a therapist. Talk about my past, my father, but I think my brain is just too busy. It chatters and barks and I find myself up late writing nonsense. I find myself wishing for love, for a guy who's less Kraft Macaroni and Cheese and more...

Torren's deep brown eyes twinkle as they meet mine. He's edgy, and raw, and it scares me. He's what I write about. He's fiction in my world of hard facts and bruised historics.

"I got twenty-five pages written, though." I keep my eyes on his and ignore how his full lips pull from his cigarette. I ignore the desire tugging on my heart, wishing I was the smoke being sucked down inside his lungs, wishing to know what it was like to be a part of him, even if it was for a few seconds.

He dashes his ash and reaches into one of the bigger pockets of his pants and pulls out a CD. "Here." He places it on the counter. "I got this for you. It will help you sleep."

The band name isn't one I've ever heard of.

"Dead Can Dance?"

His fingers smoothly push the CD case halfway across the glass, closer to me. "Yeah, bad ass album, I listen to it when I can't sleep. It helps me..." He inhales a long drag and lets the smoke pour out of his nose and mouth before he speaks again. "Helps me zone out."

Torren turns and puts his finished smoke into the ashtray.

I can't help the way my heart beats. It's fast thunder sprints and rumbles as I whisper, "Thanks."

The dark fringe of his lashes frame his bright eyes as he nods his head. "I hate that you don't sleep."

He hates...

He thinks about me.

I lick my lips and inhale. My breath is fast and he doesn't miss how it shudders.

He clears his throat, his eyes on my mouth, as he asks, "What are you doing tonight?"

I've grown used to this question. His usual friendly banter, not necessarily an invitation, but more a curious nicety one shares with the chick who works across the way from you. But he's never appraised me as he is now, like he could see through my sternum, see how my heart fluttered and hummed, how his very presence commanded my veins—my cells.

"I'm closing tonight. No big plans."

"Come by after."

His request hangs in the air like the lingering gray of his cigarette.

"To your house?" I stutter and he smiles.

"Yeah." He presses his lips together and takes a step toward the counter. "We can watch a movie or something."

Or something.

I play it safe.

Anna Josh, single white female, seeks milk toast male with no predilection for outbursts of anger. Whose mundane and routine passive personality and hobbies will keep her out of any sort of passionate argument or desire-fueled flights of fancy.

Torren Kruger is neither passive, nor mundane. He's red-hot words, and promising smiles. He's sweet and wicked, and his eyes douse me in flame. He's confidence and cock sure and, as I stand here stuck like a deer about to get hammered by a semi-truck, his knowing smile grows.

He raises his hands, his eyes dancing with possibility as he says, "I bet I can help you sleep."

I laugh openly, but my anxiety can be seen in the way I fiddle with the hem of my red cardigan. "Doubtful."

He starts to walk backward, his smile younger than his twenty-five years as he asks, "Is that a no?"

My front teeth press into my bottom lip as I try to fight my growing hope. "I don't know where you live."

"You know where Orange Street is? Off Route Sixty?"

He's almost to the entrance of the smoke shop when I answer with a nod.

He pauses and runs both of his hands through his hair, his smirk lighting fire to the paper thin lies I'm telling myself. *You don't want to go. You don't want to risk it.*

"Second house on the left," he says as he turns into the vacuous mall breezeway, the words almost lost to the echo. "See you around ten."

I didn't think of myself as a prude, or someone who didn't enjoy sex. In fact, I lovingly deemed the twenty-first year of my life the *"whore period."* Those days, my post-adolescent dream, I discovered myself. I found myself underneath the dance floor phenomenon, underneath all the gold dust, strobe light, and alcohol-induced, love-making dream. My casual encounters made my past disappear for a second of pure adrenaline. I used to love to dance. To feel like the sound was completely taking over me, like I was the only real thing left in this world. Waves of a slow beating break against the shore line, the bass a mellifluous beat, one, two, three, again and again. If I'm being completely honest with myself, I sort of miss the intimate encounters with those mysterious boys. The ones who taunted me with droopy, blue eyes and pillow-like lips. Dark yet sweet, sinister yet gentle. Those days were a blur. The sun was not your friend and the moon invited great parties. Torren's invitation though, back then I would've eaten up. But now? I'm sitting here behind the display counter chain smoking with trembling fingers just thinking over every single equation, possibility of how this... he... could be my worst idea yet.

I dash out the fiery cherry of my cigarette and lick my lips. My eyes involuntarily float across the hall again, for the millionth time, and wonder what he meant by "I can help you sleep." He was being flirty, right? The desert cracked and heated the surface of my tongue. My twenty-three-year-old brain desperately wishing the twenty-one-year-old Anna would show up to play tonight.

The thing is, I tend to hate myself. I'll overthink every last minute detail to the point of disaster. It's in times like these, where one thought perpetuates so many worries, that my eyeballs bulge with unspoken anxiety. My palms sweat, and my heart, it refuses to stay in my chest.

The sound of laughter sifts through the shop as a couple walks in. The older lady smiles at me, and my panic attack melts away for the moment as my gaze drops to the way she holds her partner's hand. Their hands are one. Linked and whole, and—right.

Stop.

Breathe.

See.

I let the air of the room filter through my lungs as I find my way back to the present, and out of the dark hole I know I'd love to drown in forever if I let myself.

I would not repeat the mistakes of my mother.

Wishing for Torren, thinking of what it would be like to have his mouth on mine, hoping his remedy for sleep was raw, physical exertion, these thoughts, they should make me feel normal, alive. I need a connection, something to prove to myself I still exist, that all the past mistakes, my father's shadow, my mother's sickness, her co-dependence do not equate to who I am. But I'm terrified of falling, and disappointment always shows up for dinner.

My mother is forever telling me to be sensible. My father told me men were evil, but we both were smart enough to figure out he was talking about himself. My sister holds to the philosophy that men are only good as friends with benefits. But what about me? A terrible sadness overflows the confines of my stomach. I've never let myself admit it, but I can't comprehend life without the chase, without the feeling there is this one special person out there just for me. My childhood was too hard, too dark to think about love. My adolescence was about survival. I never had the time to dwell on white knights or grand escapes and, as an adult, with men, I've taken the easy road every time. I could pretend I never saw it coming, never felt it make its home within the muscles of my heart, but I had let the bitterness creep in and bury itself with each relationship I've had.

"Do you have the new shipment of Cohibas in yet?" the man asks pulling me free from my neurotic brain?

The lady, maybe his wife, lets her hand release from his as she smiles at me again. I can't help but notice the deep wrinkles around her eyes and mouth and, how even though they age her, I can tell she got them from smiling all the time. From allowing happiness to soak into her skin. The thought encumbers the beat of my pulse and something heavy, but comforting, fills the space in my chest.

"Not yet, my buyer says most likely next week. If you want, leave your number, and I'll call you when they come in." My smile parts my lips as I hand him our pre-order log. "The special editions always run out so fast."

The man takes the log and begins to jot down his information with the pen I've handed him. His name is Heath. I like the feminine curve of his handwriting, the effortless feel of each letter, and I think maybe his life is just as beautiful, as easy. Once his full name and number have been scrolled across the paper, I hand him a free sample of the new cherry-vanilla pipe tobacco with the store's business card stapled to the zipped-up plastic baggy. After, the woman, whose lips stay set into a perfect, joyful, ear-to-ear smile, waves at me with her free hand over her shoulder as they leave.

I absentmindedly return the gesture and they disappear into the mayhem of the mall again. I catch a glimpse of Torren framed by the store front windows of Electronic Garden. He's watching me. His smirk is playful as he taps his watch and then walks away out of my line of sight. I turn to check the wall clock to find the day has escaped me. I'll be closing the store in about an hour and, as my eager, brown eyes seek the one thing that seems to occupy my thoughts these days, shit, this entire month, I finally decide I'm going to let myself take the fall.

A sprig of hope vines inside my heart, covering its walls and chambers, choking away the rancid and fallow surfaces. Each new branch, as I plan my night, as I imagine myself walking to his front door, knocking, dying a little when he opens it with his stunning grin and deep eyes, creates the feeling of something better. A modern day utopia where the clouds look like feathers, and I'm the kind of girl who gets what she wants, and maybe, for once, will get to sleep through the night.

***

It's eleven and I'm standing in my kitchen messing with the hem of my light gray, Red House Painters t-shirt. I'm staring at the bottle of wine on the counter. It's full and tempting, but I have to do this on my own, don't I? He's probably given up on me at this point, assuming I've bailed. But, I don't want to bail. I don't want sweaty palms and dry mouth. I want confidence. I want my legs to fucking move. I want to stop feeling nauseous, stop diagnosing myself into tidy, little compartments to condone my neuroses, stop making myself sick because I don't trust people, or myself.

"What are you doing?" my sister asks with a twitch to her lip.

She's wearing tight jeans with a halter top. She's wearing the damn confidence I wish I had.

"I'm going out," I mutter as I grab my keys from the counter with one hand while wiping the other on my jean-clad thigh. Unlike Stacey, my jeans are baggy, worn, with holes and frayed hems.

Stacey rolls her eyes with a smile as she points to the unopened bottle of wine. "You drinking that some time tonight?" I shake my head. "Can I have it? I'm meeting up with John."

I lift my chin and run my hand through my burgundy-colored hair. The strands brush my cheeks as they fall back into place along the line of my jaw. "It's all yours."

Stacey's smile holds secrets about the night ahead of her as she lifts the bottle and places it in her oversized purse. "Thanks," she says with a wave of her fingers as she turns to leave. She pauses in the kitchen doorway. "Where are you going?" Her brow quirks into a surprised question mark. As if what I said earlier is just now hitting her.

I don't go out. I am as permanent as the stains in our couch from the party she had last year. I am as steadfast as the brick and mortar of this very house. No, I don't go out. I hide and write and never sleep. I live and breathe, and forget who I am or who I wanted to be. This is my definition and I want to rewrite it.

"A guy from work asked me over," I say with my eyes fixed to the tan and brown ceramic tile floor.

"Shit, yeah?"

She isn't being mean. Stacey is my blood. She worries. I've been up and down enough she's found my routine. But I've been more down than up lately and I guess she noticed.

"Yeah." I raise my gaze to find her smile is small.

"You're wearing that?" She eyes my saggy jeans and shapeless tee.

I take a deep breath, reminding myself again, she isn't being mean. "This is who I am, Stace."

She sighs. "True story. Be careful, okay?"

I nod and, as she leaves through the garage door, I consider her words. *Be careful.* She didn't ask his name, where he lived, or even his number. I don't even have his number. Stacey either had full trust in mankind, or she didn't think I'd follow through. I ignore the slight twinge in my gut telling me she might be right.

But I've decided, instead of listening to the CD Torren gave me and helplessly trying to fall asleep, I'm taking the leap.

It's not more than a five minute drive to his house. My stomach does an excited flip at the fact he lives so close. His house is small, painted white with black shutters. A rundown and rusted Pontiac sits in the driveway. Only a few windows spill a buttered yellow light from behind drawn curtains. I swallow my nerves and the thickness of my anxiety clogs my throat as I kill the engine.

His gravel driveway crunches and the sound lingers in the heavy and humid Florida air as I approach his front door. My stiff muscles breathe as I get closer, smiling at the familiar sound of Tool sifting through his front door. Torren is a notorious diehard for the band, and just thinking about how animated he'd get when he analyzed the lyrics of their songs had my cheeks hurting with a face-splitting grin as I knock on his front door.

Instead of thinking about sweet things like a normal girl, my mind seems to take its usual path. My smile wavers as each unanswered second ticks by. Maybe he won't answer the door. What it if his invite was rhetorical, like one of those things you say all the time but don't actually mean? The thunder of my heart drowns out the music and that ever-present darkness clouds my peripheral vision. Panic. As much as I hate it, it keeps me safe. If there isn't risk then I can't ever get hurt.

When the door opens, I almost don't believe it. It's not unlikely that I could've conjured his smiling eyes and lopsided grin.

"Didn't think you were coming," he teases and runs his hand through his dark chocolate hair.

"I debated it."

He steps to the side and waves me in. The muscles in his forearms flex and he catches me staring. His chuckle unravels the knots inside my stomach and shoulders as I step past him. His arm brushes mine and his scent curls around me. The warm smell of incense and tobacco eases my breathing. His front door shuts and the permanence of it echoes through the small living room. His television is on, but muted, playing some movie I don't recognize. The furnishings are mismatched giving off a consignment shop vibe.

"It's not much," he says close enough I can feel his breath on my cheek. His soapy smell is more evident as he leans in again. "Want a drink?"

He walks past me to the kitchen which is just off the living room. An open bottle of vodka and club soda sit on the breakfast bar.

"Sure," I say lamely and follow him with small, unsure steps. "You live here alone?"

He laughs and shakes his head. "No... It's my mom's place, but she's never here, lives with her boyfriend. Stops in to pick up shit from time to time, but I pay the bills and half the mortgage so she lets me do what I want." I hesitate and his smile dims. "Lame, right? Twenty-five and still living with my mom."

"No," I say and he cocks his brow. "I'm being serious, you live here alone most of the time, right? Pay for stuff, it's not like you're mooching."

He grins. "Not a mooch."

"Then it's not lame."

"I'm hoping to get my own place. Just have to save up enough for a deposit," he says as he grabs a glass from the cabinet and fills it with ice from the freezer.

I don't say anything as I watch him pour my liquid courage into the glass. He hands me the drink without the flare of a lime or a lemon. He appraises me as I take an awkward sip. The liquor burns my tongue and the bitterness churns inside my shaky stomach. My smile is polite as I thank him and ask, "Where's yours?"

He nods his head toward the hall, and I turn my head automatically to look. "In my room."

The word room makes my cheeks flame.

"Oh," I say and gulp down another cringe-inducing sip.

Torren's laughter pulls my attention away from the music-filled hallway. "I forgot to grab limes at the store. It's terrible, right?"

An honest giggle bubbles up my throat. "It's pretty bad."

"Come on," he says and takes my hand.

Every thought I have ceases to exist as his rough hand touches my skin. It feels just as good as I hoped. I don't have time to fall into the feeling as I leave my drink and confidence on the counter. He leads me down the hallway, and I desperately wish I had something interesting to say. Some music news, or some deep, intellectual fucking anecdote to rattle off, but instead my limbs feel too rigid and my mouth too dry.

His room is as small as the rest of the house. The twin bed sits against a back wall that's littered with band posters. The only other thing besides a dresser is a computer desk. The screen is lit and setting a pale blue glow across the dingy looking carpet. Music plays from the speakers and Torren only lets go of my hand for a second to turn off the tunes before linking our fingers once again. I don't mind the tiny space or the threadbare carpet as I picture Torren spread out on his bed, and wondering if I'll be next to him soon. My mind is spinning with scenarios. What does he have in mind, what did I?

Before I can go into full-blown panic mode again, Torren picks up his drink from his dresser and asks, "Should we watch a movie?"

My stomach is bottomless as I answer, "Okay."

He treats me like this isn't my first time in his domain, like this isn't our first out-of-the-mall-experience, like I'm not dying inside, and that his touch is everything I've ever wanted and feared at the same time.

In the living room he releases my hand and sets his drink on the coffee table. He unceremoniously plops down onto the worn-out sofa and grabs a remote as he orders with a sexier-than-should-be grin, "Sit."

I'm a robot, and I wonder if he notices. He flips through the channels as the silence mounts between us. I wish I could lie back, take his hand again. Relax. As if he can hear what I'm thinking, he rests his hand on my thigh just above my knee.

"I don't bite."

I roll my eyes at his cliché line and laugh letting the tension fade. I bump his shoulder with mine and he squeezes my leg.

"I'm nervous, I guess." My eyes are still trained on the television, but I can see his smile growing wide out of the corner of my vision.

"It's just me," he says and I finally face him.

My chest aches as my heart races for the win. He tugs on a strand of my hair, his thumb grazing the skin of my jaw, and I'm held captive by the deep color of his eyes.

"That's the problem."

His head falls back as he laughs, "Oh, yeah?"

I nod and I can't help the smile that parts my trembling lips. "Yeah. You're a little forward."

"And that's bad?" he asks as he leans back into the cushions of the couch.

My eyes ingest the tight fit of his plain black tee, the way his jeans hug his thighs as he unwinds next to me.

"I'm not used to it."

"I like you," he says it with a shrug as he sits up, takes a sip of his drink, and turns the volume up on the television.

The words *I like you, too* hide behind my lips as he channels surfs, eventually settling on *Silence of the Lambs.*

"This is my favorite movie." My voice is barely audible, my throat still twisting up with his declaration.

His brown eyes meet mine, and I want him to move his hand higher, or maybe just hold mine again. His hand slides off my knee and the disappointment cools my fevered pulse.

"Top five favorite, for sure," he says turning his gaze slowly away from me and to the movie.

We sit quietly for a few minutes as Anthony Hopkins drills Jodie Foster about the night she ran away from her uncle's farm. For a blessed few seconds, I forget I'm sitting next to a man who smells like temptation. I forget that I'm always nervous around him, and how I don't feel good enough or pretty enough. I just sit and, when Torren shifts his body, I don't even look. I'm in my own private bubble.

When he speaks again, I almost jump. "Lie down."

I turn to see he's sprawled out behind me on the couch. His one arm supporting him, and his other resting along the side of his body. It feels too intimate of an invitation, but his lips are lifted and sweet and his eyes expectant, and I give in settling down next to him.

My back is against the firm plane of his chest, and his arm is wrapped around my waist. I swear when he pulls me closer I feel him breathe in and out deeply, his breath tickling my ear. His fingers toy idly with the hem of my t-shirt, his thumb occasionally dusting the bare skin of my hip above the waistline of my jeans. Goosebumps spread across my skin and my eyelids flutter closed.

This is unlike any date I've ever been on. There are no awkward questions or small talk because I already know him. I know his favorite band is Tool, and that he prefers Marlboro Reds. I know that he used to live in Delaware and that he wants to be a computer programmer. Did I know everything? No. But I like how easy this is, how the slow rhythm of his fingers tames me. I've always been afraid of my own heart and, with him, since I've met him, all I seem to want to do is unleash it. Remember that I once wished I could have this great something and neverending anything. And even though this was a beginning, maybe it was a step in the right direction.

We stayed like that all night as we watched the movie. Never needing to fill the air with useless chatter. His breathing became my breathing, and the light lull of his fingers eventually put me to sleep. The heat of his body kept all my monsters away, and I actually fucking slept. When I found myself awake in his arms I wished I could've stayed there forever. I recognized the need in his eyes when I turned to meet his own sleepy gaze. My lips begged to be kissed, to sip from his mouth, but his hand had only held my cheek as he asked, "Will you be okay to drive home?"

My fingers hesitate, my key still inside the lock of my front door as I think about how his eyes had devoured me. Every muscle in my body rebels. Anxiety storms through my pulse, but instead of feeling sick all I want to do is run. Run fast and hard until I'm back at his doorstep, knocking on his door and demanding that he kiss me, maybe even claiming his mouth without giving him the choice. I want to know what he tastes like, if his lips were soft or firm. If he'd groan, run his hands through my hair, or grip my waist. My heart is an incessant hammer as I pull his number from my pocket. I bite my lip and bring my fingertips to my mouth as I hear his voice in my head.

"Come over tomorrow?"

A slight edge of worry colored his tone when he asked me. I smile at the absurdity of Torren Kruger nervous with his sexy grin and sleep-tousled hair.

I let the key twist in the lock as I promise myself in a whisper, "Tomorrow."

If this isn't love...

His hands are tomorrow and they're breaking me down. Dissecting me into smaller pieces so he can savor the time. There isn't anything between us except for soft sounds and sweat and I'm lit at both ends. The words *"maybe we should wait"* are tossed on the floor with my oversized t-shirt and jeans. His mouth is telling me it's all going to be worth it as he tastes my lips. His body is hard and it overwhelms me, fills me and makes me speak in a language I'm not sure existed before he and I were one.

There was no time for movies or small talk. The minute he opened his door in low-slung jeans and no t-shirt he knew what he had in mind. His forward ways were set in high definition as he framed my face with his hands and kissed me like he was starving. His hello stifled by my sigh of relief and the way my bones melted, only he was strong enough to carry me.

And he did, right to his room.

I could stay here for all eternity if he keeps me pinned like this, keeps me in kisses and feeling and sex.

"Open your eyes," his hoarse whisper commands and I listen.

I'm met with dark eyes rimmed with amber sin and I'm falling. His hand cups my breast then finds its way between my legs and, when I shatter, it's all for him. It's for the way his jaw constricts and his body cages mine. It's for the way he touches his forehead to my brow with a growl and grips my hips as he stills inside me. It's for the way he kisses me like I'm spread too thin, and his tender lips fear the destruction of his own kiss.

My eyes are wide open, and I whisper with a shiver as his hair brushes against my cheek. "Hi."

His chuckle makes me laugh and he groans as he slips away, breaking our connection. "Hi," he repeats and turns to his side. He wipes the damp strands of my hair from my face and his smile annihilates me. He's sated and watching me like I'm the last person he'll ever smile at ever again.

Maybe I'm easy and foolish to fall for a man I barely know beyond his thirty-minute smoke breaks and *The Silence of the Lambs* with a side of vodka. But he makes it easier to sleep, he make it easier to feel like I might still have some sort of spark, some brightness left inside me. Maybe I'm naïve to put too much faith in one person, but in this moment, covered in his scent and heat, I allow myself the indulgence.

"Do you work in the morning?" he asks as his fingertips trail along my collarbone, down my chest and along the curve of my breast.

The blue light of his computer is the only thing illuminating the room and casts shadows across his face making it hard to read his features. "No," I answer as I run my fingers through his hair. The thick locks are exactly how I imagined, and I lean my head to the side and inhale his scent.

"Then sleep over." It isn't a question and I don't miss the way my body tingles with anticipation of a possible round two.

"You realize we talk more at work than we have tonight, or last night, for that matter."

His laugh is full and my lips break into a smile in response.

"It's not my fault you fell asleep last night," he teases and begins to draw those same sleep-inducing circles on my stomach.

Goosebumps erupt under his touch. I'm lying on my back, naked and vulnerable and the same phrase keeps repeating over and over and over in my head, before I can stop it I blurt, "Are we a thing?"

His nose nuzzles into my neck just below my ear and, Torren Kruger, my mysterious mall guy crush, says with a bit of his own vulnerability, "We've been a thing for a while, I think."

I want to tell you that this is the guy... the "*him*"... the one who gave me a second chance at living. I want to tell you that this moment with Torren was the first and last best thing to have happen to me, but I can't.

I can tell you we had a good run. That I reveled in feeling wild, and sexy and worshipped. That Torren opened up a side of me I never knew was fighting to get out. I can tell you that after a year with him I never wanted another man to touch me again, that he evoked such sensations that I was sure no other man would ever compare. After a year I was head-over-fucking-heels in love with him, in love with the idea of how far I'd come, in love with the idea of us.

Trust me, I don't want to tell you about the night he asked me over for dinner, and fucked me right before he told me he wanted to break up. I don't want to tell you that he cheated for at least four of those glorious twelve months. I don't want to tell you how I felt used, and disgusted and confused. I was fifteen all over again and wondered how I had been so wrong, and how the hell I'd found my way back to rock bottom.

The thing I do want you to know, that I must tell you... is that Torren Kruger almost destroyed me.

Almost.

Life always boiled down to a choice: sink, swim, or float. And if I'm being honest, I drowned for about a month. I even managed to sleep with the asshole again. I debased and devalued myself in hopes he might change his mind. I'd hit an all-time low...again. I was terrified of losing the power I'd found within myself, and I was angry because it was all tied to him. Or so I thought.

For a while I floated. Forty-eight days of keeping my head above water, and when I grew sick of how everything in my hometown reminded me of him and his stupid fucking hair, and smile and goddamn face, I packed everything I owned into my small hatch back, road tripped across the country and found a temporary home with my other sister in Utah.

There was no giving up, no more razor blades, if I can thank Torren for anything, it was that he rattled my cage. I took a chance and I can say I am glad I did. He shook up my complacent little bubble and showed me what it felt like to burn. Even though he'd left me in ashes, scorched and over used, as cliché as it sounds, it gave me the opportunity to rise again. And every wall I hit for the next fifteen years, and there were many, I took stock in the fact that I knew the landscapes of rock bottom. All-time-low had a distinct flavor and, for a while, it was all I could taste. But, everything the universe sent, I could survive, because each ledge, each pitfall, each mountain of ash I fell into, I knew I could find my way out because I've done it before. And each time it was less painful.

I'm thirty-eight years old, and my skin is written with so many scars. I've chosen to wear them like a soldier wears a Purple Heart. My life has wounded me, but I've learned that I am not defined by the marks I've gained over the years. I am built by them, beautiful and strong and because of them—the good things—the happy moments—are that much better.

The end...

His hand rests against the soft curve of my belly as he pulls my back to his chest. He smells like the spice of his cologne and his beard tickles the back of my neck as he places open-mouthed kisses to my shoulder. We spent the last thirty minutes talking about soccer practice on Saturday, and how we were supposed to balance between Eden's and Aaron's games. I mentioned how well David did today in play therapy, and my husband promised he'd make the next appointment. But now, the world is silent as his lips remind me that there is more to life than calendars and carpool and, here in his arms, I never have to think about anything other than how good it feels to be loved. My eyes close as he rolls me onto my back and kisses me with gentle lips. He's feather soft at first, then demanding as the heat melts away his gentlemen's mask. There is nothing for me to worry about as his hands touch me. After eight years of marriage, sometimes we have to work hard for these quiet moments.

His mouth becomes greedy, and I let my eyes open. Eric's too busy sampling my skin to notice the split second of darkness that I accidently allow to flicker across my gaze. I will always harbor that blue flame. No matter how much I've healed, it scatters shadows from time to time. My soul had been haphazardly pieced together, but it matches his. I love how human he is... how imperfect. When I was younger, I wanted to put my faith in others, in men, and never myself. I needed for someone to tell me I was good enough to be loved, and sometimes I still do, but after all these years I've figured out the only way to get off the ledge is to pull *yourself* up.

He traces my bottom lip with the pad of his thumb as he whispers, "I'm right here."

My past, my mistakes, they have been silenced. Our bed is for forgetting, and the happy ache in my chest swells as he reminds me like he does every night.

Thank you for reading.

Special thanks to Alissa for telling me, day in and day out, I have what it takes. Sometimes I don't believe you, but on the days I do, I'm blessed with a pen that won't stop moving.

www.ingramcontent.com/pod-product-compliance
Lightning Source LLC
Chambersburg PA
CBHW031625040426
42452CB00007B/674